CANCER SCORPIO PISCES

TAURUS VIRGO CAPRIC

INTUITIVE ARTISTIC QUICK LEARNING NURTURING EMPATHETIC PASSIONATE EMOTIONAL DEEP SELF-PROTECTIVE OBSESSIVE

PHYSICA... ... DRIVEN PATIENT MATERIALISTIC

WATER

♋ ♏ ♓

CANCER: YOU ARE IMAGINATIVE, SENTIMENTAL AND LOYAL

SCORPIO: YOU ARE RESOURCEFUL, BRAVE AND TRUTHFUL

PISCES: YOU ARE ARTISTIC, GENTLE AND WISE

EA...

♉

TAURUS: YOU ARE DETERMINED, RELIABLE AND PRACTICAL

VIRGO: YOU ARE MODEST, HARDWORKING AND SUCCESSFUL

CAPRICORN: YOU ARE WISE, SELF-CONTROLLED AND ORGANISED

GEMINI: YOU ARE ADAPTABLE, SOCIABLE AND AFFECTIONATE

LIBRA: YOU ARE SOCIABLE, BALANCED AND CO-OPERATIVE

AQUARIUS: YOU ARE INDEPENDENT, SOCIABLE AND ORIGINAL

ARIES: YOU LIKE WORKING YOUR BODY HARD AND BEING IN CHARGE

LEO: YOU HAVE A PENCHANT FOR EXPENSIVE THINGS

SAGITTARIUS: YOU LOVE THE GREAT OUTDOORS AND TRAVELLING

SOCIABLE KNOWLEDGEABLE ANALYTICAL FICKLE EXPRESSIVE CREATIVE KNOWLEDGEABLE PHILOSOPHICAL INTELLECTUAL

INSPIRATIONAL CONFIDENT IN CONTROL EXPLORERS TRAILBLAZERS FUN, EXCITING ENTHUSIASTIC ACTIVE

♊ ♎ ♒

AIR

♈ ♌ ♐

FIRE

GEMINI LIBRA AQUARIUS

ARIES LEO SAGITTARIUS

First published by **FROM YOU TO ME LTD** November 2022

To personalise journals and books as well as purchase other gifts, please visit

WWW.FROMYOUTOME.COM

FROM YOU TO ME are committed to a sustainable future for our business, our customers and our planet. This book is printed and bound in China on FSC®certified paper.

1 3 5 7 9 11 13 15 14 12 10 8 6 4 2

ISBN 978-1-907860-82-9

Born In The 40s

Do you remember...

home security

hot water rationing

having your sweets weighed

outside toilets

the nit nurse

that's the way to do it!

home delivery

the birth of Rock 'n' Roll

the school bell

homemade transportation

walking to school whatever the weather

Sunday best

these springing up

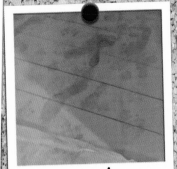

dust everywhere

days out

jam sandwiches

street parties

pond dipping

target practice

clocks going forward 2 hours in summer

POST OFFICE TELEGRAM

Charges to pay
RECEIVED
at Central Telegraph
Office, E.C. 1.
Prefix. Time handed in. Office of Origin and Service Instructions. Words.
99
From. 21.03.1954 To.

ABSOLUTELY LOVING MEMORY LANE BOOK.
DON'T WANT IT TO
EVER. STOP.

prams left outside

milk to your door

freedom on two wheels

The Memory Times

THE FRUGAL FORTIES!

As the 1940s began, the world was in the throes of World War Two, a period which those who lived through will never forget. The UK started the decade not only with the introduction of food rationing, which would last for longer than many had anticipated, but also sub-zero temperatures that led to the freezing of the River Thames in London for the first time since 1888. Winston Churchill was appointed as Prime Minister in 1940 the same year The Battle of Britain took place, which was pivotal in the outcome of the war.

1941 saw the introduction of the Woolton Pie, a vegetable pie named after the Minister for Food, due to rationing and a shortage of meat. The Morrison Shelter was introduced for people without garden air raid shelters, and it could double up as a kitchen table. The National Fire Service was established in August 1941, initially created to put out fires and rescue the injured during bombing raids.

In 1942 the radio programme Desert Island Discs invited 'castaways' to choose 8 pieces of music, a book and a luxury item that they would take to an imaginary desert island. Most people chose soap as their luxury item, which at the time was a luxury item for everyone as it was rationed.

Resources became thin on the ground in 1943 so the government introduced Utility Furniture to ensure the production of strong, well-designed furniture that made efficient use of timber. New furniture was restricted to newlyweds and people who had been bombed. Pigeons White Vision, Winkie and Tyke became the first recipients of the Dickin Medal, introduced to honour the work of animals in wartime.

The London Olympic Games were postponed in 1944. The PAYE system of tax collection was introduced, and the unfair prohibition of married women being allowed to be schoolteachers ended.

With the war coming to an end in 1945, street parties took place all over the country. Winston Churchill made his victory speech and appeared on the balcony of Buckingham Palace. On the last day of 1945, Britain received its first shipment of bananas since the beginning of the war.

1946 saw the BBC resume its television broadcasting, having shut down in 1939, with the introduction of the £2 annual television licence. League football began again, and the jitterbug dance craze swept across the country. Free milk to school pupils was announced to better nourish the nation's children.

The school leaving age was increased to 15 in 1947. Sadly, the BBC had to suspend their television service once again as power supplies were interrupted during a particularly severe winter. Thankfully, they were back in time to broadcast the marriage of Princess Elizabeth to Philip Mountbatten, whose engagement had been announced just after her 21st birthday (they had secretly got engaged the year before!).

In 1948, even though many householders' shopping lists were still limited by rationing, the first supermarket was opened by the London Co-operative Society in Manor Park. Satisfying the nation's sweet tooth, Rowntree created the Polo mint, whilst the first Land Rover was unveiled at the Amsterdam Motor Show. Most importantly, the new National Health Service offered the right to free universal health care for all.

As the decade drew to a close in 1949, Longleat House became the first stately home to open its doors to the public on a fully commercial basis, 16 years before becoming a safari park. George Orwell's dystopian novel Nineteen Eighty-Four was first published, depicting a time in the future where states put their citizens under surveillance, with Big Brother always watching.

THE FABULOUS FIFTIES!

The 1950s was a high-octane rock and roll explosion. Many recording artists pioneered this new and exciting form of music, giving young people a genre of their own, and allowing post war teenagers a real identity for the first time. The end of fuel rationing in 1950, resulted in the first Silverstone Grand Prix and the very first package holiday air charter being introduced by the Horizon Holiday Group.

With more cars back on the roads, possibly listening to the newly launched The Archers radio programme, 1951 saw the introduction of zebra crossings to make it easier for people to cross the road.

In 1952, radio listeners could enjoy the new UK Singles Chart published by the New Musical Express, whilst others could sit down with a nice cup of tea to watch black and white TV. The first TV detector van was commissioned this year to catch anyone that didn't pay their licence fee!

The rationing of sweets finally ended in 1953, significantly increasing the need for fillings which at the time involved drilling out most of the tooth and filling it with an attractive grey metal amalgam. Watch With Mother aired for the first time and Ian Fleming published the first James Bond novel, Casino Royale. Following the untimely death of her father King George VI, in 1953 the world saw the ascension and coronation of Queen Elizabeth II at Westminster Abbey.

In 1954, Roger Bannister became the first man to run a mile in under 4 minutes. He didn't have to worry about sprinting to the front of any rationing queue as in that same year all rationing ended. Oxford won the 100th boat race and radio comedy series Hancock's Half Hour aired for the first time.

Halfway through the decade in 1955, record-breaking Stirling Moss won the British Grand Prix, whilst that same year the Guinness Book of Records launched. A new television channel called ITV, to compete with the BBC, was started.

Young people enjoyed the new UK Album Chart, which was introduced in 1956. They were also able to take part in the new Duke of Edinburgh Awards scheme, but this was only for boys! Just as the UK had got used to no rationing, back it came in the shape of fuel rations due to the Suez Canal Crisis.

In 1957, people rang the BBC in their droves to ask how they could also grow their own spaghetti trees, after watching a special Panorama report on the Swiss Spaghetti Harvest. It was, of course, the first ever April Fool's joke to be played on national television! The same year saw the opening of a little venue in Liverpool, The Cavern Club, that would play host to then little-known names, such as Gerry and the Pacemakers, The Searchers, Cilla Black, The Beatles, and The Rolling Stones.

Motoring was again the theme in 1958, when parking meters were introduced and work on the M1 motorway, designed to make driving long distances easier and more pleasant for motorists, started. Disaster struck in 1958 when an aircraft carrying the "Busby Babes" aka the Manchester United football team crashed in Munich, resulting in 23 fatalities with 21 survivors.

1959 saw the launch of a new mode of transport - the hovercraft. Initially rejected by the Navy as they deemed it to be an aircraft and rejected by the Air Force as they deemed it to be a boat, this invention was a big success, and consequently transported over 80 million people across the channel between England and France. Britain signed the North Atlantic Treaty, creating NATO in the same year. Lastly, in 1959 the continuing saga of rock and roll opened a new chapter, when a young Jimi Hendrix bought his first electric guitar. The Fifties were indeed fabulous!

YOU ARE WHAT YOU EAT

MENU

TASTE OF THE PAST DINER – YOU ARE WHAT YOU EAT

DRINKS

SCHOOL MILK - Warm bottles of milk served with a layer of warm cream.

RETURNABLE FIZZY POP - Sparkly sweet beverage, wondrously presented in a 1 litre bottle. Remember to hand empties back to your waiter in exchange for cash.

TEA - One spoonful for each person and none for the pot! So say the Ministry of Food during the war. By 1950, 55% of children drank this beverage!

CORPORATION POP ON THE ROCKS - Natural, locally sourced beverage. Completely free from flavouring, colouring, aroma and price. Served from a twist handle dispenser. Ice made from the same liquid.

MAINS

FISH FINGERS - New to the menu (1955). Our confused chef wonders which breed of fish actually has fingers.

GO TO WORK ON AN EGG - One egg is an oeuf.

LORD WOOLTON'S PIE - Named after the Minister for Food, this vegetable soup in a pie will be quickly forgotten when conditions return to normal. (If you can't finish it, don't throw it away, the council road sweeper will collect it to feed the animals.)

QUICHE LORRAINE - A beautiful layered feast, starting with a hard layer of unmelted cheese, followed by soft clammy grey egg peppered with rubber bacon and soggy pastry.

WHITE BREAD SANDWICH WITH BEEF PASTE - Limp, almost damp, white bread made from bread and plastic, designed to stick to the roof of your mouth, lovingly filled with tuna-flavoured beef spread. Also available: tuna-flavoured chicken, tuna-flavoured ham, and cardboard-flavoured tuna.

BURGER 'N' MILKSHAKE - New American-influenced dish! Fry-days and Sundaes only.

SCHOOL DINNER SURPRISE - Sausages browned only on one side leaving the rest pink. Served with a side of green stuff that might be peas, and an ice cream scoop of grey mashed potato. The 'surprise' is it actually tastes worse than it looks.

CORONATION CHICKEN - To order this dish, please take a seat at the long trestle table filled with your neighbours. Outside in the street.

POP QUIZ

1 Sweet rationing started in 1942. How many ounces was the sweet ration per head ?

2 In which year was sweet rationing lifted?

3 Weston's launched Wagon Wheels biscuits in 1954. How big was it in inches?

1. 8oz 2. 1953 AND BRIEFLY 1949 3. THREE AND A QUARTER INCHES

KIT KAT
CONTROLLED PRICE
2½D EACH
PRODUCT GROUP C1

Because no milk can be obtained for chocolate manufacture, the Chocolate Crisp you knew in peace-time can no longer be made. This is the nearest possible product at the present time.

TEMPORARY WARTIME PACKING
CONTENTS REMAIN UNCHANGED

2ᴅ Pkt
POTATO SMYTHS

The GI's arrived in 1941, and a phrase of the time was "They're over-fed, over-sexed, and over here!"

K CHOCOLATE

MENU

TASTE OF THE PAST DINER - YOU ARE WHAT YOU EAT

STARTERS

CHEESE AND PINEAPPLE STICKS - Six-sided 'government cheddar cheese' portions nestled with tropical fruit, coupled with a delicate birch skewer, dried and hardened for several hours.

JACKET POTATO PETE - "Those who have the will to win, cook potatoes in their skin, knowing that the sight of peelings, deeply hurts Lord Woolton's feelings!"

VICTORY VEG - Carrot and swede juice 'Carrolade', as much as you can stomach. We've got loads of this due to 'daylight savings' being put forward by 2 hours for extra farming time.

DESSERTS

TRIO OF PUDS - 3 delicious choices: Tapioca (AKA Frogspawn), Spotted Dick (AKA Fly Cemetery) and Lumpy Custard (AKA Cat Sick with Skin).

BLANCMANGE - Like a flavoured sandcastle the tide couldn't destroy if it tried.

JUST A SPOONFUL OF SUGAR - Please queue up at the front to be administered cod liver oil, malt extract, polio sugar cube and welfare orange. One spoon fits all. One spoon per queue.

~~BANANA~~ **CAKE** - Just cake. Bananas out of stock until 1946.

INSTANT POWDERED PUD - A light, gentle, magical dust, transformed with milk and sugar into a light, gentle, magical dust with milk and sugar.

SIDES

A LITTLE EXTRA ON THE SIDE - Food too 'hot' to handle, fresh from under the counter, sourced from your local (black) market. Until 1955.

NATIONAL LOAF WITH DRIPPING - Grey, gritty, mushy loaf. Actually improved by adding dripping.

A PACKET OF PORK SCRATCHINGS - Actually only half a packet, as 50% of every pig goes to the government. Unless it's unregistered, in which case, tuck in!

FISH 'N' CHIPS - This may be a main course, but as these have not been rationed, you can have a portion on the side!

WORD OF MOUTH - Alphabet - spaghetti. Enough for approximately 6 to 8 swear words per serving.

6% OF HOUSEHOLD BUDGETS WERE SPENT ON CIGARETTES IN 1952

Treats For The Adults

BABYCHAM
SNOWBALL
WORTHINGTON'S
BABY BUBBLY
MILK STOUT
VP RICH RUBY
PORT & LEMON
DUBONNET
BASS
GOLD LABEL

YUMSTICK

MAYBE GLAM

Sparkling

COOPE
UBLE
MOND

AT BURTON

BARRAT
RATION BAG

CONTAINING SWEETS
NUTS, POPCORN, ETC

Treats For The Kids

RATION CHOCOLATE PARMA VIOLETS
COLA CUBES FRY'S FIVE BOYS
PEAR DROPS SPANGLES
PINEAPPLE CHUNKS LIQUORICE
CANDY CIGARETTES LOOT BAGS
ANISEED BALLS NOUGAT
MINT IMPERIALS TIFFIN
CATHERINE WHEELS GOBSTOPPER

HANDMADE FUN

ARMPIT FART

"HERE'S THE CHURCH AND HERE'S THE STEEPLE"

CLAPPING GAMES

MIDDLE FINGER TRICK

See see my play mate . . .
A sailor went to sea sea sea . . .

SCHOOL FIELD DAY

CUT GRASS FIGHTS

STICKY WEED

DO YOU LIKE BUTTER?

DAISY CHAINS

HERE'S A TREE IN SUMMER...

GRASS WHISTLE

CONKERS

PLAITING HAIR

HANDSTANDS

DANDELION CLOCK

BUNDLE

Pile up as many people as possible.
Bottom two layers go straight to nurse's office.

JUMPERS FOR GOALPOSTS

A game of football with no limit on numbers, no rules and no referee. Take injured to nurse's office.

ORANGES AND LEMONS

"Here comes a chopper to chop off your head . . ."
Take player who ends on that line to nurse's office.

TAG **A.K.A. IT, TIG, ETC**

The game that doesn't end until one, or all players get hurt. Take injured to nurse's office.

WHO'S IT?

ROCK, PAPER, SCISSORS

SHORT STRAW

ONE POTATO, TWO POTATO, THREE POTATO . . .

EENY, MEENY, MINY, MO

After a morning of working hard, sitting crossed-legged in assembly and trying not to laugh at the kid in the 'spare shorts' who'd pee'd himself (again), lunch would be bolted down in the dinner hall until finally it was time for freedom in the great outdoors.
The games of the playground were the perfect training arena for the real world, both the good and the bad. Break time consisted of a mixture of semi-violent activities, slightly questionable games, politically incorrect insults and the multiple uses of hands. Many games ended in tears and a trip to the nurse's office. All decisions were made with 'eeny, meeny, miny, mo' and other tried and tested methods.

"First the worst. Second the best, third the one with the hairy chest!"

BRITISH BULLDOG

Run across playground without being rugby tackled. Take injured to nurse's office.

HIDE AND SEEK

The seeker searches and the hiders hide amongst stinging nettles, up in a tree, or by a wasps' nest. Take injured to nurse's office.

KISS CHASE

Spend the whole of break chasing each other, until tooth collides with head. Take injured to nurse's office.

LEAP FROG

Try to jump over someone without booting them in the face. Take injured to nurse's office.

PLAYGROUND TOYS

PAPER FORTUNE TELLER

YOYO

JACKS

FRENCH SKIPPING

MARBLES

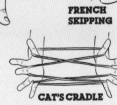

CAT'S CRADLE

LOVE LETTER

Grazed knees, grass-stained clothes and scuffed shoes were the look of the day. On summer days the water fountain was used for cooling down. School ties were yanked, hoods became superhero capes, on windy days coats were held above heads like sails, and everyone remembers the day a dog roamed into school.
All too soon an end to the fun would be signalled by a teacher ringing the bell and everyone would line up and shuffle back into the toxic-tiled lead-painted pre-fab classroom, planning what to do in the NEXT playtime...

'HARMLESS' FUN

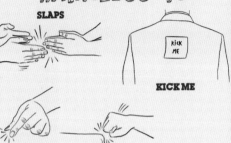

SLAPS

KICK ME

PINCH, PUNCH, 1ST OF THE MONTH

KNUCKLES

THUMB WAR

DEAD ARM DEAD LEG

SLAP HEAD

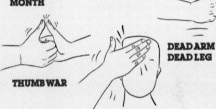

SPITBALLS

ARM BURN

HEADLOCK

WEDGIE

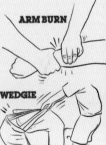

PLAYING ARMY

ARM WRESTLE

MONDAY

Norman And Henry Bones The Boy Detectives
Henry Bones voiced by Pat Hayes . . . that's PatRICIA Hayes, who went on to voice other boy characters 'Ginger' in 'Just William' and 'Master O.K. the Saucy Boy' in 'What Sauce'.

Radio Ventriloquism?!
Educating Archie
Albert Daveen & Daisy May
A.C. Astor
Coram & Jerry
Johnson Clark
Arthur Prince & Jim

Woman's Hour
Today's programme:
'How to Improve Your Whatnot'
"MuuuUUUuuum? What's a whatnot?"

Mrs Dale's Diary
Soap opera.
Today, Jenny has measles, but listeners complain in their thousands that she already had measles in 1949. The writers should have checked their diary. Meanwhile, Mary is still 'rather worried about Jim'.

The Story Of Dr Kildare
In today's episode, Dr Kildare is forced to perform an emergency appendectomy on himself, but the operation is cancelled at the last minute because the doctor is unwell.

Hancock's Half Hour
'Sunday Afternoon at Home'. It's raining at 23 Railway Cuttings. "You watch. It'll go dark in a minute. We'll have to switch the lights on. I think I'll go to bed." Sounds like a typical Sunday. In August.

Take It From Here
Featuring The Glums.
Today, Mr Glum tries to extract another pint from the landlord, whilst recounting the week's goings on of his son Ron and his long-term fiancée Eth.
In this episode, Ron mistakes his nose for the coin slot at the launderette.

TUESDAY

Children's Hour
14th October 1940.
A very special presenter today . . . Princess Elizabeth addresses the nation's children!
Maybe she'll try and get Uncle Mac to change 'Storm of Green Hillocks' from a sheep dog to a corgi?

Housewives' Choice
"Doodle-dum-de-doodle-dum."
George Elrick sings his own, possibly quickly-written lyrics over the theme tune.

Gardeners' Question Time
From the seeds of 'Down the Garden Path' bloomed 'How Does Your Garden Grow', resulting in this evergreen radio programme.

The Archers
Actress Monica Gray campaigns for equal pay, and coincidentally in today's programme, her character Grace goes up in smoke in a barn fire. What bad timing.

Send For Paul Temple
If you are a criminal, and you suddenly get an invitation to a gathering thrown by private investigator Paul Temple, then "by Timothy" DON'T GO!

Stand Easy
'Tarzan of the Tapes' featuring Charlie Chester.
"Down in the jungle, living in a tent, better than a prefab – no rent!"

Crazy People
Spike Milligan, Harry Secombe, Peter Sellers and Michael Bentine team up in this surreal comedy. What a goon show.
Now THERE's an idea for a title . . .

Twenty Questions
Episode finishes early tonight, as Gilbert Harding tells listeners "I'm fed up with this idiotic game, I'm going home". Producers consider removing gin from the dressing rooms.

WEDNESDAY

Listen With Mother
"Are you sitting comfortably? Then I'll begin." Stories, poems, songs and rhymes, and the latest tale about 'My Naughty Little Sister'.

Music While You Work
Upbeat tunes to encourage factory workers to speed up. Industrial bosses are pleased when a freak power surge speeds up the BBC gramophone, and triples their output for the day.

Cookery
Bearded chef Philip Harben introduces us to the delights of scampi. A young Captain Birdseye listens intently and takes notes . . .

Under Milk Wood
Starring Richard Burton, who is obviously a milk fan, as he later marries Liz Taylor who famously takes a bath of asses' milk as Cleopatra.

A Life of Bliss
George Cole had a very different life as David Bliss, long before leading a life of dodgy dealings as Arthur Daley.

How Do You Do
Arthur Askey broadcasts live … from your home!

ITMA (It's That Man Again)
Featuring catchphrases including "It's being so cheerful as keeps me going" by Mona Lott, "Can I do yer now sir?" by Mrs Mopp and "I don't mind if I do" by Colonel Chinstrap.

The Navy Lark
Leslie Phillips commands "Left hand down a bit", while Jon Pertwee yells "Everybody down!" followed by a loud crash. Meanwhile, Ronnie Barker answers the phone with "'Ello, intelligence 'ere."

A Case For Dr Morelle
In this episode, does Dr Morelle treat his secretary Miss Frayle in his usual chauvinistic way? "Remember, you are the judge."

TIME

THURSDAY

Toytown
Fed up with his short stature, Mr Mayor asks the magician to make him 'big', but he mishears and turns him into a 'pig'.

Top Of The Form
Inter-schools quiz. In the literature round, child contestants battle it out answering questions on 'Sense and Sensibility'.

Workers' Playtime
Variety show live from a factory canteen. The BBC transports crew, cable, microphones, two pianos, two pianists, a producer and a group of variety artists up and down the country, three times a week, to boost morale. Today's show comes from a Sheffield steel works and handily features comedian Stainless Stephen.

Radio Crossword
1 Across: Wireless cryptic quiz programme (9,5)
A: Programme Title

Beyond Our Ken
Comedy, featuring characters including Fanny Haddock, Hankie Flowered, Ricky Livid and Arthur Fallowfield.

Merry-Go-Round
"Week by week this show goes around the services, bringing music and fun to the boys and girls in khaki, and two shades of blue", leading to spin offs 'Much-Binding-in-the-Marsh', 'Waterlogged Spa' and 'Puffney Post Office'.

The Piddingtons
Sydney and Lesley read each other's minds. On the radio. "Telepathy or not telepathy? You are the judge." Did we place this programme directly next to the one on the left because it has the same catchphrase?

FRIDAY

The Adventures Of Dan Dare
"Spaceships Away", to deliver discs of the latest episodes from London to Luxembourg for broadcast.

Music And Movement
For today's memorable exercise class, it's over to Ann Driver: "We're going to play a hiding and finding game. We'll pretend you have some balls, and I'm going to hide them. Are they up high near the ceiling? Or down low so you have to pick them up off the floor. You don't know where I'm going to hide your balls. Now dance lightly about looking everywhere for your balls. Now you've found them, toss them in the air and play with them."

Two-Way Family Favourites
The time in Britain is twelve noon, in Germany it's one o'clock, but home and away it's time for "Two-Way Family Favourites!" Meanwhile, Jean Metcalfe and Cliff Michelmore strike up a secret romance behind the scenes…

The Brains Trust
Practical and moral matters answered by a team of experts. Today, the burning question that everyone needs an answer to: "How does a fly land on a ceiling? Does it loop the loop or what?"

Hi Gang!
Entertainment show hosted by radio rivals Ben Lyon and Bebe Daniels, but don't worry, in real life they're the husband and wife team behind Life with the Lyons.

Up The Pole
Sitcom set at an Arctic trading post, starring Jimmy Jewell, Ben Warriss and Jon Pertwee, who would later be back up a pole as Worzel Gummidge.

SATURDAY

Children's Favourites
"Hello, children everywhere." Derek 'Uncle Mac' McCulloch plays requests from young people. It's more exciting hearing your name read out than the song you requested!

Dick Barton - Special Agent
Omnibus edition in case you missed any of the weeknight 6:45 shows. Today, once again, Barton's crime-busting gadgets do the trick. "With one bound, Dick was free!"

Mystery At Witchend
When David, Peter, Mary, Dickie and Tom form the Lone Pine Club, they're determined to have lots of adventures. When they start bumping into strangers in the hills and the friendly Mrs Thurston begins acting oddly, they realise something mysterious is going on.

Kitchen Front
Cooking and housekeeping tips. Today, the 'Radio Doctor' Dr Charles Hill dispenses health advice whilst smoking a pipe.

Chance of A Lifetime
Dick Emery gives contestants another chance to win £30 to spend in a Marshall Ward catalogue. Teenage boy winner goes straight to the underwear page.

Variety Play House
Tonight the show plays out to The Nutcracker Suite, to help fill any extra time left of this live show.

In Town Tonight
"Once more we stop the mighty roar of London's traffic and, from the great crowds, we bring you some of the interesting people who have come by land, sea and air to be In Town Tonight." Tonight featuring Tommy Trinder, "You lucky people."

SUNDAY

Charles Chilton Double Bill
Riders of the Range:
A group of heroes saddle up and prepare to explore the barren landscape of the wild west.
Journey into Space:
A group of heroes buckle up and prepare to explore the barren landscape of the Moon.

Jennings At School
Today will Jennings describe Mr Wilkins' anger as "Ozard", "Ozard squared" or "Ozard cubed".

The Billy Cotton Band Show
Wakey WAAAAAAAAAAAAAKEEY!

Desert Island Discs
Today's castaway is Sally Ann Hawes, who chooses garlic as her luxury item. Luckily, she's marooned alone.

Have A Go
Wilfred Pickles gives members of the public another chance to win the £1/18/6d jackpot. "What's on the table Mabel?" "Give 'em the money Barney!".

Ray's A Laugh
Ted Ray's catchphrase-filled comedy show. "It was agony Ivy". "I'll have to send for young Dr Hardcastle". "He's lovely Mrs Hoskins, he's loooooovely".

Listen To The Band
The only occasion when listening to the military's top brass harping on and blowing their own trumpets is music to your ears.

Variety Bandbox
Philip Slessor brings us more new acts for our enjoyment. Tonight, a comedian new to radio with the catchphrase "Ye may titter. Titter ye may". Can you name him?
A: Frankie Howerd

GAME ON!

42 Pet knocked over Domino line up GO BACK 3 SPACES

43 Baking Powder Submarine sprung a leak GO BACK 14 SPACES

44

45 Finally managed to throw Yahtzee! ROLL AGAIN

40 Played Risk, conquered the world! THROW AGAIN

39

38 Your last battleship sunk! MISS A GO

37

36

21

22 Muffin the Mule's strings tangled up MISS A GO

23 Got Bayko building set for birthday! ROLL AGAIN

24 Silly Putty

25

20 Didn't get a tiddlywink in the pot MISS 2 TURNS

19

18 Managed a beard and moustache on Wooly Willy ROLL DICE AGAIN

17 Passed 'GO' in Monopoly MOVE ON 4 SPACES

16 Dartboard on wall. Dart in wall. Oops! BACK TO START

GO!

2

3 Hit finger with hammer playing Tap Tap BACK TO START

4 Who is this, launched in 1952?

5 Made a tin can & string telephone – it worked! MOVE TO 13

ANSWER: Mr Potato Head (Required a real potato!)

46
Didn't buzz in wire and loop game
MOVE ON 1 SPACE

47

48
Managed a successful neck spin with Hula Hoop
ROLL AGAIN

49
Meccano structure collapsed
MISS A GO

Finish!

35
Clock broke in Beat The Clock
GO BACK 3 SPACES

34

33
Rain didn't wash hopscotch away
1 MORE THROW

32
Slinky

31
Spinning Top didn't fall off the table
MOVE ON 1 SPACE

26
Flipped Scalextric car on corner again
GO DOWN SNAKE

27

28
Safely manoeuvred in Remote Control Driving Test
MOVE ON 1 SPACE

29
TOKEN FOR ARCADE ONLY NO CASH VALUE

30 ?
Cluedo launched in 1949. Can you name all six murder weapons?
ANSWER: Candlestick, Dagger, Lead Pipe, Revolver, Rope, Wrench.

15
Airfix Golden Hind bag ripped. Piece missing!
MISS A GO

14
Metal horse missing from Totopoly set
NEXT ROLL GOES BACKWARDS

13

12
Magic 8 Ball gives unwanted answer
MISS A GO

11

6
Used a 'Z' tile in Scrabble
ROLL AGAIN

7
Lost slinky race down the stairs
MISS A GO

8
Spilt water over Paint By Numbers!
MISS 2 TURNS

9
Found missing jigsaw piece under sofa!
MOVE ON 2 SPACES

10

MATCH THE DANCE TO THE MUSICAL!

1. SINGIN' IN THE RAIN 1952   A. THE WATER BALLET
2. ANCHORS AWEIGH 1945   B. 'GOOD MORNING' SOFA DANCE
3. BATHING BEAUTY 1944   C. JERRY MOUSE & GENE KELLY TAP
4. YOU WERE NEVER LOVELIER 1942   D. THE SHORTY GEORGE

Musical Youth

SING-A-LONG-A-WAR QUIZ

IN THE SONG 'WHITE CLIFFS OF DOVER'
WHAT IS THE NAME OF THE BOY WHO WILL GO
TO SLEEP IN HIS OWN LITTLE ROOM AGAIN?

'WE'LL MEET AGAIN' WAS A FAMOUS
HIT BY WHICH WARTIME SINGER?

NAME THE TWO PLACES IN LONDON MENTIONED IN THE SONG
'IT'S A LONG WAY TO TIPPERARY'.

FLANAGAN AND ALLEN CHANGED A POPULAR SONG'S LYRICS TO
'RUN ADOLF, RUN ADOLF', BUT WHAT WERE THE ORIGINAL WORDS?

BANNED ON THE RADIO BANDS!

SONG: I'M ALWAYS CHASING RAINBOWS.
REASON: THE BBC WANTED TO GET RID OF SONGS THAT WERE CONSIDERED TO BE
"SICKLY SENTIMENTAL". THEY FELT SUCH MUSIC WOULD LOWER THE MORALE
OF A WAR-TORN NATION.

SONG: DEEP IN THE HEART OF TEXAS.
REASON: JUDGED TO BE SO JAUNTY THAT IT WAS BANNED FROM THE AIRWAVES IN
CASE FACTORY WORKERS DOWNED THEIR TOOLS TO CLAP ALONG WITH THE SONG.

SONG: MINNIE THE MOOCHER.
REASON: CONTAINED DRUG REFERENCES AND "LOOSE MORALS".

JAZZ HANDS

Are these jazz musicians from the UK or the USA?

UK / USA — LOUIS ARMSTRONG
UK / USA — BILLY HOLIDAY
UK / USA — GLENN MILLER

UK / USA — KEN COLYER
UK / USA — ACKER BILK
UK / USA — ELLA FITZGERALD

ANSWERS IN GREEN!

1950s RADIO FACTS

IN 1955, THE BBC BROADCAST IN FM FOR
THE FIRST TIME, AS A SUPERIOR ALTERNATIVE
TO AM WHICH WAS SUSCEPTIBLE TO INTERFERENCE
IN BAD WEATHER.

IN 1954, THE WORLD'S FIRST COMMERCIALLY MANUFACTURED
TRANSISTOR RADIO, THE REGENCY TR-1, WENT ON SALE.
IT WAS PORTABLE AND CHANGED THE WAY PEOPLE LISTENED TO RADIO.

THE BBC SOUND EFFECTS UNIT, THE RADIOPHONIC WORKSHOP,
OPENED IN 1958. IT PIONEERED THE USE OF ELECTRONIC MUSIC,
CREATING THEME TUNES SUCH AS DOCTOR WHO.

50s ROCK & ROLL QUIZ

1. WHO PERFORMED THE ORIGINAL VERSION OF 'HOUND DOG'?

2. WHO WROTE 'BLUE SUEDE SHOES'?

3. WHO HAD A HIT WITH THE SONG 'ROCK AROUND THE CLOCK'?

4. IN WHICH YEAR DID THE EVERLY BROTHERS RELEASE 'WAKE UP LITTLE SUSIE'?

5. WHO HAD A HIT WITH THE SONG 'GREAT BALLS OF FIRE'?

6. UNSCRAMBLE THE LETTERS TO REVEAL THIS 1950s ROCKER.
CYIRK SLNOEN

DID YOU KNOW?
THESE ACTS STARTED OUT IN 50S SKIFFLE BANDS!

MICK JAGGER
VAN MORRISON
ROGER DALTREY
BARRY GIBB
JIMMY PAGE
THE BEATLES

CAN YOU REMEMBER
THESE 1950S CROONERS?

ANDY WILLIAMS
NAT KING COLE
BING CROSBY
FRANK SINATRA
PERRY COMO
TONY BENNETT
DEAN MARTIN
PAT BOONE
AL MARTINO
SASHA DISTEL
ENGELBERT HUMPERDINCK
JOHNNY MATHIS
FRANKIE LAINE
DON CORNELL

Top 50s Singles

NO CHARTS	**TENNESSEE ERNIE**
1950	1955
NO CHARTS	GIVE ME YOUR WORD
NO CHARTS	**DORIS DAY**
1951	1956
NO CHARTS	WHATEVER WILL BE WILL BE
AL MARTINO	**PAUL ANKA**
1952	1957
HERE IN MY HEART	DIANA
FRANKIE LAINE	**THE EVERLY BROTHERS**
1953	1958
I BELIEVE	ALL I HAVE TO DO IS DREAM
DORIS DAY	**RUSS CONWAY**
1954	1959
SECRET LOVE	SIDE SADDLE

ROCK & ROLL QUIZ ANSWERS:
1. BIG MAMA THORNTON
2. CARL PERKINS
3. BILL HALEY AND HIS COMETS
4. 1957
5. JERRY LEE LEWIS
6. RICKY NELSON

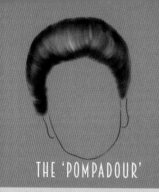
THE 'POMPADOUR'

THE 'PAGE BOY'

THE 'NIT NURSE'

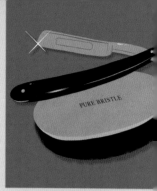

THE 'SIDE PARTING'

SLICK 40s LOOKS

THE 'MOVIE ICON'

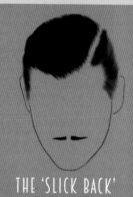
THE 'SLICK BACK'

THE 'BACK ROLL'

WITH RATIONING IN FULL EFFECT, WOMEN HAD TO CONTEND WITH A SHORTAGE OF HAIR PRODUCTS INCLUDING SHAMPOO, AND WITH MANY WORKING ON THE LAND AND IN FACTORIES, HEAD SCARVES AND SNOODS BECAME THE ORDER OF THE DAY. WHEN PERFECTING A 'DO', SETTING LOTIONS WERE MADE FROM SUGAR WATER OR EVEN BEER, AND HAIR WRAPPED IN RAGS OR NEWSPAPER. THEY STILL LOOKED FABULOUS! FOR THE MEN AND BOYS, HAIR WAS A SHORT BACK AND SIDES, WITH A POMADED SIDE PARTING OR SLICKED BACK LOOK. SOME EVEN EMULATED ICONS FROM PREVIOUS ERAS, WITH A CLARK GABLE PENCIL MOUSTACHE OR AN ERROL FLYNN WAVE ON TOP.

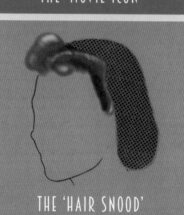
THE 'HAIR SNOOD'

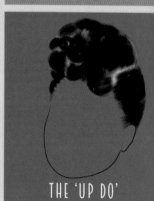
THE 'UP DO'

PEEK-A-BOO BANGS

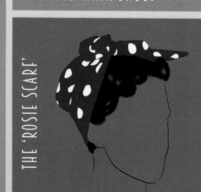
THE 'ROSIE SCARF'

PIN CURLS

The 'Quiff'

The 'Grace Kelly'

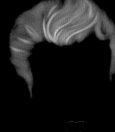

The 'Greaser'

The 'James Dean'

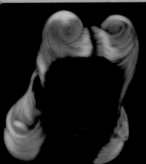

Hair Rollers

Thick Fringed

Rocking 50s Looks

The 'Pin Up'

The 'D.A.'

The 'Monroe'

KIDS IN THE 50s WANTED THE HAIR OF THEIR FAVOURITE MUSIC AND FILM STARS, AND ACHIEVED THIS IN MANY WAYS. HAIR WAS PINNED, GRIPPED, IRONED, TIED UP WITH RIBBONS AND FILLED WITH CURLERS (EVEN WHILST SLEEPING!). BOYS USED A VARYING AMOUNT OF OILY, GREASY, WAXY PRODUCTS TO GET THE PERFECT ROCK N ROLL QUIFF WITH A MATCHING DUCK'S TAIL AT THE BACK, EVEN USING CHEMICAL GELS THAT STRAIGHTENED HAIR WHILST BURNING THE SCALP! BUT AS LONG AS YOU LOOKED COOL AT THE LOCAL JIVE HALL, THAT'S ALL THAT MATTERED DADDY-O!

The 'Poodle'

The 'Croft'

The 'Hepburn'

High Tail

ROYAL CROWN POMADE

TOMORROW'S World Today

DUCT TAPE
1943. Originally called 'Duck' tape and invented for keeping ammunition boxes waterproof during World War Two, this handy invention has been holding pieces of tech together ever since.

AEROSOL
The 'Bug Bomb' spray can helped US soldiers fight malaria in the Pacific from 1941.

POLAROID CAMERA
The first Polaroid camera, called the Model 95, and its associated film, went on sale in 1948.

MICROWAVE OVEN
In 1945, Percy Spencer invented the microwave by accident, whilst working on magnetrons for radar sets, and his candy bar melted in his pocket.

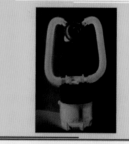

AQUA-LUNG
The first open-circuit, self-contained underwater breathing apparatus, invented in France in 1942.

LP RECORD
In 1948, created by Peter Goldmark, this vinyl record had a capacity of around 21 minutes per side and was 12 inches wide, playing at a speed of 33 1/3 RPM.

ELECTRONIC DIGITAL COMPUTER
Colossus was the world's first electronic digital programmable computer, and was instrumental in the decoding of messages during the war. It was shipped to Bletchley Park on January 18th 1944 and attacked its first message on February 5th.

JET ENGINE
Frank Whittle's turbojet engine performed its first test flight in 1941.

DIALYSIS MACHINE
The first type of dialyser, then called the artificial kidney, was built in 1943 by Dutch physician Willem Kolff.

COLOUR TV
Colour commercial broadcasting began in 1953.

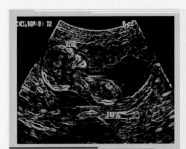

ULTRASOUND
Used in Glasgow hospitals in the 1950s.

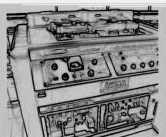

VIDEO TAPE RECORDER
The Ampex VRX-1000 was the first commercially successful VTR.

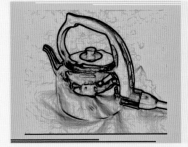

AUTOMATIC KETTLE
Russell Hobbs launched in 1955, the first electric kettle to switch itself off once boiled.

TEASMADE
Started to become very popular in the late 1950s.

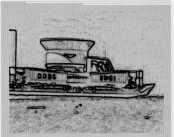

HOVERCRAFT
Saunders-Roe SR.N1 - this practical hovercraft performed its first public flight in 1959.

PACEMAKER
First implantable pacemaker in 1958.

SOLAR BATTERY
Bell System announced in 1954.

DISK DRIVE
IBM 350 was the first secondary storage for computers.

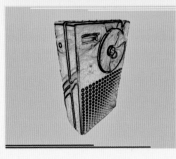

TRANSISTOR RADIO
The Regency TR-1 was the first commercially manufactured transistor radio, introduced in 1954. The transistor component was invented at Bell Laboratories in 1947.

LIGHTS.CAMERA.ACTION...

SCREEN 1940s
GREAT FILMS BY YEAR

19:40	PINOCCHIO
19:41	SERGEANT YORK
19:42	BAMBI
19:43	THIS IS THE ARMY
19:44	GOING MY WAY
19:45	BRIEF ENCOUNTER
19:46	BLUE SKIES
19:47	AN IDEAL HUSBAND
19:48	BRIGHTON ROCK
19:49	SAMSON & DELILAH

SCREEN 1950s
GREAT FILMS BY YEAR

19:50	CINDERELLA
19:51	ALICE IN WONDERLAND
19:52	THE GREATEST SHOW ON EARTH
19:53	PETER PAN
19:54	REAR WINDOW
19:55	LADY & THE TRAMP
19:56	REBEL WITHOUT A CAUSE
19:57	THE BRIDGE ON THE RIVER KWAI
19:58	SOUTH PACIFIC
19:59	CARRY ON NURSE

CINEMA TICKET

ADMIT ONE

1940 price: 10d - 4.37p
1950 price: 1/6d - 7.54p

40s & 50s

HOW MANY OF THESE HAVE YOU WATCHED?

SCI-FI

FLASH GORDON CONQUERS THE UNIVERSE
DR JEKYLL AND MR. HYDE
SUPERMAN
MYSTERIOUS ISLAND
HOUSE OF DRACULA

INVASION OF THE BODY SNATCHERS
THE DAY THE EARTH STOOD STILL
THE INCREDIBLE SHRINKING MAN

HORROR

THE CAT PEOPLE
THE WOLF MAN
THE BODY SNATCHER
THE UNINVITED
I WALKED WITH A ZOMBIE
THE FLY
CREATURE FROM THE BLACK LAGOON
THE BLOB
DRACULA
THE MUMMY

...IT'S SHOWTIME!

ROMANCE

BRIEF ENCOUNTER
CASABLANCA
NOTORIOUS
THE PHILADELPHIA STORY
REBECCA

THE SEVEN YEAR ITCH
SEVEN BRIDES FOR SEVEN BROTHERS
ROMAN HOLIDAY
THE AFRICAN QUEEN

ANIMATION

FANTASIA
THE JUNGLE BOOK
ALICE IN WONDERLAND
DUMBO

1001 ARABIAN NIGHTS
WHAT'S UP DOC?
CINDERELLA
PETER PAN
ALICE IN WONDERLAND
ANIMAL FARM

ACTION

HENRY V
THE TREASURE OF THE SIERRA MADRE
RED RIVER
SHE WORE A YELLOW RIBBON
THE MARK OF ZORRO
THE THREE MUSKATEERS

HIGH NOON
GUNFIGHT AT THE O.K. CORRAL
THE DAM BUSTERS
DAVY CROCKETT AND THE RIVER PIRATES

KIDS

LASSIE COME HOME
MY FRIEND FLICKER
NATIONAL VELVET
THE ENCHANTED FOREST
THE SECRET GARDEN

TREASURE ISLAND
20,000 LEAGUES UNDER THE SEA
THE 7TH VOYAGE OF SINDBAD
TOM THUMB
AROUND THE WORLD IN 80 DAYS

FANTASY

IT'S A WONDERFUL LIFE
THE BLUE BIRD
THE BOY WITH GREEN HAIR
BEAUTY AND THE BEAST
I MARRIED A WITCH

JOURNEY TO THE CENTRE OF
THE EARTH
BRIGADOON
THE 5,000 FINGERS OF DR. T.
CAROUSEL
BELL, BOOK AND CANDLE

THRILLER

ODD MAN OUT
BLACK NARCISSUS
THE THIRD MAN
OUT OF THE PAST
SPELLBOUND
THE STRANGER

STRANGERS ON A TRAIN
REAR WINDOW
VERTIGO
TO CATCH A THIEF
STAGE FRIGHT

DRAMA

CITIZEN KANE
THE MAN IN GREY
GREAT EXPECTATIONS
ARSENIC AND OLD LACE
DOUBLE INDEMNITY

THE KING AND I
REBEL WITHOUT A CAUSE
CAT ON A HOT TIN ROOF
SUNSET BOULEVARD

COMEDY

LET GEORGE DO IT!
SPARE A COPPER
KIND HEARTS AND CORONETS
MIRACLE ON 34TH STREET
MEET ME IN ST. LOUIS

GUYS AND DOLLS
ANNIE GET YOUR GUN
SOME LIKE IT HOT
FUNNY FACE

1. WHO WAS IT THAT SAID, "PLAY IT, SAM, PLAY 'AS TIME GOES BY'," IN THE 1942 MOVIE "CASABLANCA"?

2. WHICH COMEDY TEAM STARRED IN THE 1943 FILM, "JITTERBUGS"?

3. IN THE 1945 FILM "BRIEF ENCOUNTER" A MARRIED WOMAN MEETS A STRANGER, AND THEY EMBARK ON AN EMOTIONAL LOVE AFFAIR. WHERE DO THEY MEET?

ANSWERS:
1. INGRID BERGMAN
2. LAUREL AND HARDY
3. A RAILWAY STATION

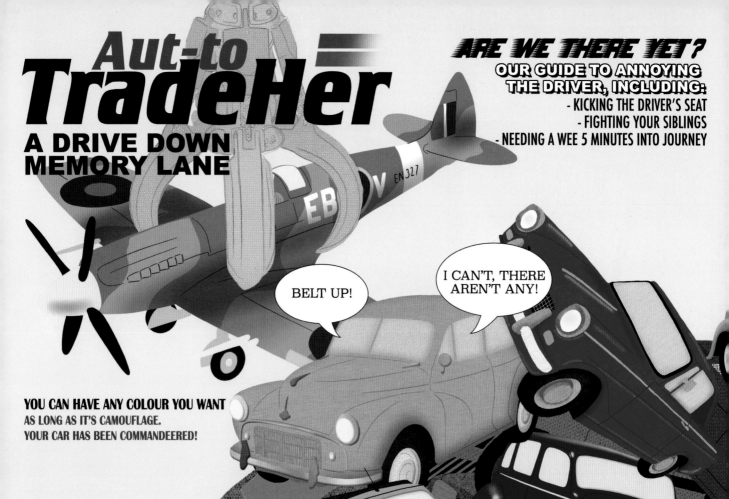

SUMMER HELL-IDAY!

HOW I SURVIVED VINYL SEATS IN SHORTS,
A NON-OPENING WINDOW, AND 8 HOURS OF I-SPY.
ONE READER'S TERRIFYING TRUE STORY

MANE ATTRACTION
YOU'VE BOUGHT A NICE SHINY NEW
HILLMAN MINX, BUT THE KIDS ARE MORE
EXCITED TO SEE THE RAG AND BONE
MAN'S HORSE. AGAIN.

POLICE

POLICE

ONE FOR THE ROAD:
DON'T FORGET TO ADD A
MEASURE OF OIL WHEN
YOU FILL UP!

BUBBLE TROUBLE
KNOCK KNOCK. WHO'S THERE? NO ONE.
NEW BUBBLE CAR PARKED IN FRONT OF A
BRICK WALL WITH NO REVERSE GEAR!

I'LL TURN
THIS CAR AROUND
IF YOU DON'T
BEHAVE!

SERVICE

CLOSE SHAVE!
Scraped your shin on a
rusty running board.
Thank goodness tetanus
shots have been
introduced!

DAYLIGHT ROBBERY!
HOW ONE PENSIONER'S TRIP TO THE
SHOPS COST HIM HIS FREEDOM:
TRAFFICATOR POP-UP INDICATORS STUCK
OPEN, AND COLLECTED 14 HANDBAGS,
TWO TERRIERS ON LEADS, AN OLD LADY'S
SHOPPING TROLLEY AND A POLICEMAN'S
HELMET IN ONE SHORT JOURNEY.

YOU CAN'T GET-TIN!
...TO THE TRAVEL SWEETS TIN...
AND IF YOU DO...THE WHITE
POWDER'S GOING EVERYWHERE!

ORI-CAR-MI
THE MAP'S TOO BIG FOR THE CAR INTERIOR...
AND IT'LL NEVER FOLD BACK UP!

Your CHINESE New Year!

RAT
Imaginative	Shrewd
Generous	Cynical
Successful	Critical
Popular	Hoarder
Curious	
Sociable	

OX
Confident	Set in their ways
Honest	Possessive
Patient	Brutally honest
Thorough	Stubborn
Innovative	
Determined	

TIGER
Sensitive	Over-indulgent
Tolerant	Easily distracted
Brave	Complacent
Active	Emotional
Resilient	
Charismatic	

RABBIT
Affectionate	Overly sensitive
Kind	Pessimistic
Gentle	Easily scared
Modest	Avoids problems
Empathic	
Trustworthy	

DRAGON
Enthusiastic	Needs boundaries
Intelligent	Brutally honest
Lively	Whimsical
Energetic	Unfocused
Innovative	
Spiritual	

SNAKE
Enthusiastic	Unpredictable
Intelligent	Insensitive
Romantic	Greedy
Polite	Lazy
Elegant	

HORSE
Diligent	Short-tempered
Intelligent	Stubborn
Friendly	Selfish
Talented	Over-confident
Reliable	
Courageous	

GOAT
Artistic	Easily upset
Calm	Pessimistic
Happy	Repetitive
Reserved	Over-protective
Caring	
Sensitive	

MONKEY
Witty	Annoying
Flexible	Irritating
Lively	Egotistical
Humorous	Temperamental
Curious	
Versatile	

ROOSTER
Shrewd	Possessive
Motivated	Over-protective
Punctual	Indecisive
Flexible	Arrogant
Confident	
Honest	

DOG
Loyal	Super sensitive
Honest	Nervous
Responsible	Needs support
Lively	Cold
Smart	
Sociable	

PIG
Sincere	Over-sensitive
Tolerant	Stubborn
Honest	Naive
Honourable	Materialistic
Determined	
Optimistic	